SAI

SAI

KARATE WEAPON OF SELF-DEFENSE
by
Fumio Demura

Library of Congress Catalog Card Number: 74-83597

ISBN 0-89750-010-5

Thirty-second printing 2001

Graphic Design by Geraldine Simon

OHARA ⓪ PUBLICATIONS, INCORPORATED

SANTA CLARITA, CALIFORNIA

ACKNOWLEDGEMENT

I would like to express my thanks to Mr. Gary Hallenbeck and Mr. Yoji Sakumoto for their selfless assistance in the preparation of this book. Also, a great debt of appreciation is owed to Mr. Ed Ikuta for his excellent and patient photographic skills.

DEDICATION

To the one person initially responsible for my interest and knowledge in kobudo, the late Okinawan master Kenshin Taira, and to the one person who motivated me as my personal instructor, Ryusho Sakagami.

ABOUT THE AUTHOR

Fumio Demura, 5th-dan, was born in Yokohama, Japan. He began his martial arts training during his grammar school years when he studied the art of kendo as a means of building up his strength and improving his health. When his teacher moved from the area, Mr. Demura was relocated to another dojo which taught both karate and kendo. He then studied aikido in high school and, later, judo. While at Nihon University in Tokyo, from which he received a Bachelor of Science Degree in Economics, he developed interest in all the martial arts, including the techniques of such weapons as the bo, sai, tonfa, kama and nunchaku, which he perfected under the tutelage of Mr. Kenshin Taira and Mr. Ryusho Sakagami.

Noted in Japan as an outstanding karateka, Demura has been honored by martial artists and government officials alike. In 1961 he won the All-Japan Karate Free-Style Tournament and was lauded as one of Japan's top eight players for three consecutive years (1961-64). His tournament wins have been numerous, including the East Japan, Shito-Ryu Annual and Kanto District championships. He received the All-Japan Karate Federation President's trophy for outstanding tournament play and has

received certificates of recognition from such Japanese Cabinet officials as the Ministers of Education, Finance and Transportation for his outstanding achievements and contributions to the art of karate.

In response to an invitation by Mr. Dan Ivan, Fumio Demura came to the United States in 1965 to teach Shito-Ryu—one of the four major systems of karate in the world. He now heads his own dojo in Santa Ana, California and supervises instruction at the University of California at Irvine, Orange Coast College and Fullerton State College. In addition, he is the director of the Japan Karate Federation in the United States and advisor for the Pan-American Karate Association.

Besides his full-time job as an instructor, Demura has taken on a strenuous demonstration schedule at Japanese Village and Deer Park in Buena Park, California, where his exhibitions have become an important part of the park's attractions.

In 1969, the BLACK BELT MAGAZINE Hall of Fame paid tribute to the author's dedication to karate with its coveted Karate Sensei of the Year award. Mr. Demura's first book, *Shito-Ryu Karate*, was published in 1971, closely followed by his best-seller, *Nunchaku: Karate Weapon of Self-Defense.*

HISTORY OF THE SAI

During the Japanese occupation of Okinawa some 350 years ago, invading warlords prohibited the use of ordinary weapons such as the sword or spear. So the Okinawans turned to karate and kobu-do (the use of karate weapons such as the bo, a staff; nunchaku, two hardwood sticks securely connected by rope or chain; kama, a sickle; and surushin, a length of rope with weights attached to both ends) for protection. Some kobu-do weapons were farm implements which the ingenious farmers converted into effective protective devices. For instance, the sai (short sword) was dragged through the soil by one peasant, while another would plant seed in the resulting furrow. If approached by a marauding samurai, the sai (pronounced "sigh") doubled as a weapon with which the peasant could counter a sword attack. Usually the peasant employed two sai, one for each hand, and concealed a third inside his obi (wide belt), which even a proficient sai artist may have found cumbersome when engaging in battle with a talented swordsman. Thus the third sai was actually used to throw at the warrior. This maneuver was often the key to winning the encounter.

The sai originally was capable of killing or maiming an enemy with a blow to the back of the neck or a thrust to the throat or the eyes. However, the sharp points of that first sai have been blunted and rounded. It no longer serves as a weapon for mortal combat. Fashioned of steel and chrome-plated, it is a most attractive instrument bearing two prongs at the handle.

Originally, the sai was formed from two components, the curved prong section and the main stem. These separate parts were then pounded into a unit using a process similar to that employed by Japanese swordsmiths. Approximately 100 years ago, a more progressive means for making sai was utilized. A finished sai was laid in the sand to cast an indented impression. When the sai was removed, molten lead was poured into the cavity. After the lead cooled and hardened, rough edges were ground off and the finished instrument was polished.

When first introduced to Japan, the sai was called jutte. It bore a single prong at the handle. The Japanese police found it quite effective in blocking the thrusts of the samurai. The sai was also used against pressure points when making arrests. Japanese karate practitioners at that time accorded the instrument a rather cool reception. Very few found it interesting enough to try, but once they did, they were fascinated with it.

Americans became increasingly aware of the sai when karateka (karate men) flashed it during kata (form) competition at tournaments. They promptly recognized it as a valuable instrument for developing poise and posture, so essential to good karate.

Rigid training and skill are required to manipulate the sai in techniques which parallel the movements of karate. Practitioners of the sai develop excellent flexibility in the use of their hands and can often handle the instrument with the dexterity of a majorette twirling a baton.

Skillful use of the sai requires special coordination exercises and advanced proficiency in the art of karate. For this reason, Mr. Demura recommends that a person below the rank of brown belt should not attempt to practice with the sai.

CONTENTS

ANATOMY OF THE SAI

The sai is made of chrome-plated steel and weighs one pound, 10 ounces. To give the user a better grip, a cotton ribbon over a string wrapping has been wound around the handle. To protect your arm

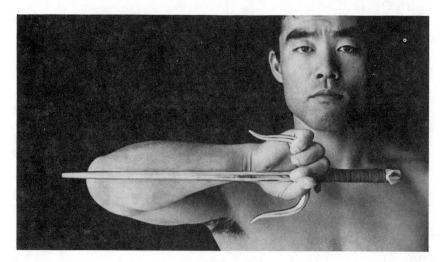

from being struck, the length of the sai should be approximately one inch past the length of your elbow. The butt of the handle is an inch beyond the tip of your index finger.

POINT

The point is sometimes sharp, but more often rounded. Occasionally, a lip or button is placed on the point making the appearance of the sai similar to a fencing foil.

BLADE

The blade is either rounded or hewn into six or eight symmetrical facets. The facetted type blade is considered the most practical. Some blades are flat like that of a sword.

PRONGS

The prongs or guards are usually curved like a trident and useful for halting the stroke of a sword or bo.

GUARD

CENTER OF BALANCE

GUARD CENTER

The guard center is the hub where the prongs meet the handle.

HANDLE

To provide a firm grip, the handle is often wrapped with cotton tape or thick string.

BUTT

The butt is designed in various shapes and can be used in the same manner as a karate punch.

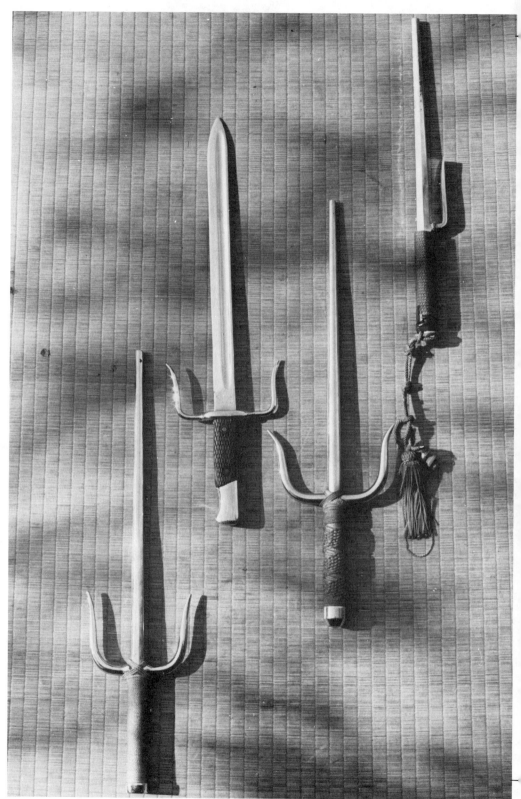

CARE OF THE SAI

Before the development of nickle and chromium plating, the iron sai had to be kept free of rust by applying plant oil. If you own a pair of sai fashioned from iron, avoid applying oil to the handle. The oil will mix with the moisture of your hands, causing the sai to slip from your grasp when practicing.

Today, because of the metal-plating processes, the application of oil is not so important, but the metal should still be wiped free of hand moisture.

GRIPPING THE SAI

There are only two ways to hold the sai. One is with the blade
pointing outward and the other with the blade pointing inward.

SIDE VIEW

BLADE OUTWARD

(1) Place the handle in your palm with its prongs at right angles to your hand. (2) Close your four fingers over the handle. (3) Place your thumb over the point where the prongs and blade intersect and tighten your grip. Placing your thumb over the guard center provides more power when blocking and striking. (Top View) Looking down, note line of your thumb is parallel to the blade.

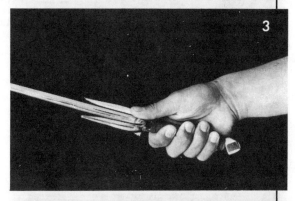

TOP VIEW

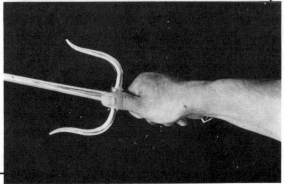

17

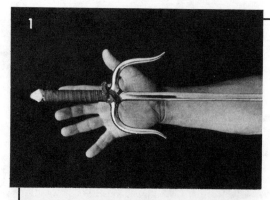

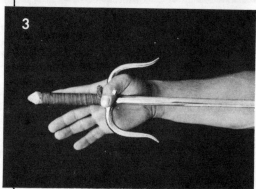

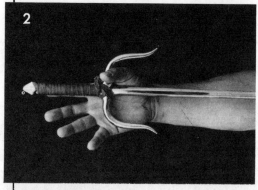

BLADE INWARD

(1) The sai should be parallel to your arm and your index finger. (2) Insert your thumb between the top prong and the blade. (3) Bend your thumb over the sai at the intersection of the prongs and blade and

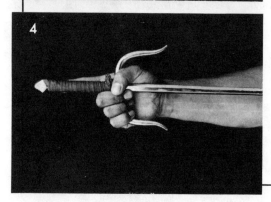

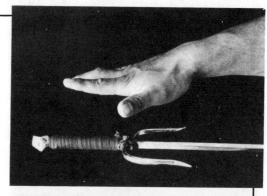

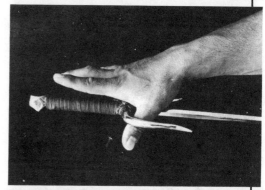

keep your extended index finger parallel to the handle. (4) Grip the lower prong of the sai with your three remaining fingers and place your thumb over your forefinger as shown.

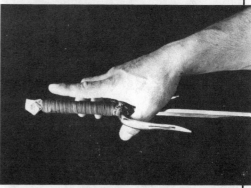

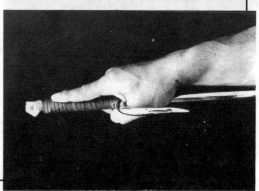

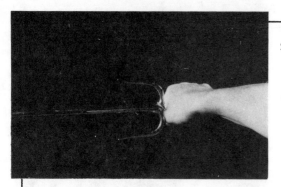

THUMB AROUND HANDLE

Assuming the blade outward grip, place your thumb around the handle of the sai. This grip can be used for both striking and blocking.

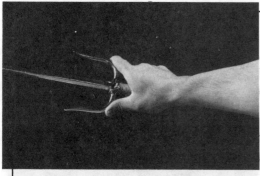

SIDE VIEW

THUMB AND INDEX
FINGER ON PRONG

Assuming the blade outward grip, place your thumb and forefinger on the prongs as illustrated. This grip is used for offensive thrusting maneuvers.

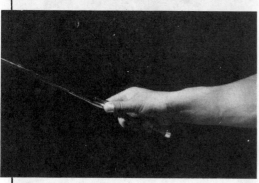

FRONT VIEW

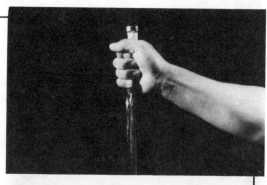

BLADE DOWNWARD

With the blade pointing downward, grip the sai with your thumb
around the handle.

FRONT VIEW

SIDE VIEW

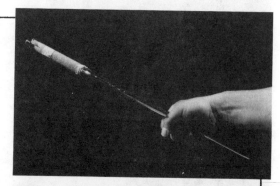

GRASPING THE BLADE

With the handle pointing slightly
upward, grip the blade of the sai. In
this position you can use the prongs
for hooking techniques.

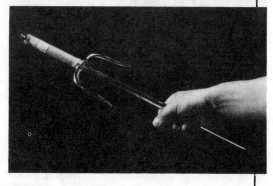

FRONT VIEW

FLIPPING THE SAI

To develop a strong kime (proper focus) with the sai at the point of impact, your wrist and elbow must coordinate in the snapping movement. This rule must be followed when using vertical, horizontal, or inside-outside movements.

Your elbow is the center of an imaginary circle, part of which your wrist circumscribes. Similar to most karate movements, the elbow, arm and wrist are kept relaxed until the moment before contact with the sai is made. At the end of the arc inscribed by the point of the sai, your grip is tightened, your forearm tensed and your elbow locked. The relaxed, natural move associated with fly casting is sought, as well as perfect coordination between the parts of the body involved. Elements of speed and control provide the desired snap.

Do not put too much body power into the snap; keep your body relaxed. Concentrated tension in your shoulders can restrict the flow of the move. The power should be concentrated in your hand. Develop the feeling of a whipping motion when flipping the sai. Professional golfers sometimes use the principle of "throwing the club head at the ball" to get the required snap. The same principle can be applied here.

Proficiency in flipping the sai can only be developed through hours of practice. The flipping movements have no real counterpart in karate, but must be learned separately by the karateka.

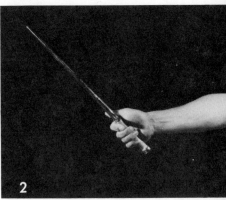

INSIDE RETRACTION

(1) Grip the sai in the blade outward position. (2) Remove your thumb from the guard center and place it between the blade and right prong. (3-5) Using a strong wrist action, flip the point backward toward your elbow. (6, 7) As the sai reaches your elbow, place your index finger along the handle.

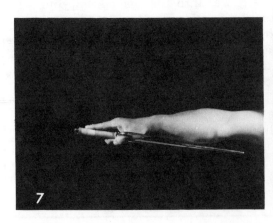

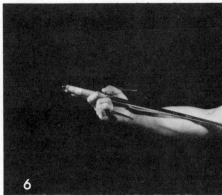

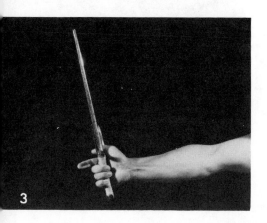

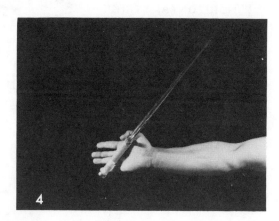

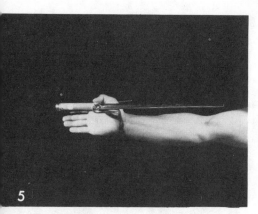

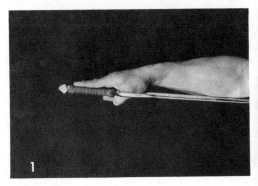

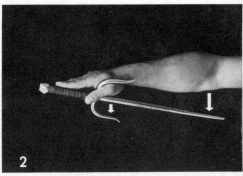

HORIZONTAL STRIKE

(1) Assume the blade inward position with your arm fully extended. (2) With your index finger remaining on the handle, straighten your last three fingers and relax your thumb. This will allow the blade to fall free of your palm and forearm. Maintaining the same hand position, (3) begin rotating your forearm and wrist to the left toward your body. (4) Continue the counterclockwise rotation (approximately 60 degrees) and begin to slide all four fingers over the handle. (5) Close your fingers over the handle and, with your thumb now on the lower part of the blade, begin a clockwise rotation to the right, using your thumb as a lever. (6) Proceed rotating your forearm clockwise with your thumb pushing the blade forward. (7) Continue the rotation to the right while tightening your grip on the handle. (8) Snap your forearm and wrist into a fully extended position as your hand assumes the basic blade outward grip.

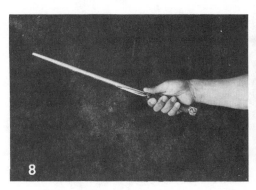

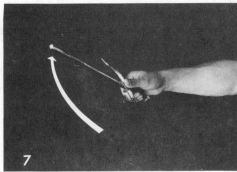

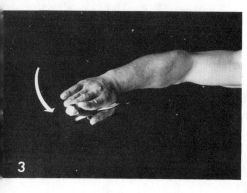

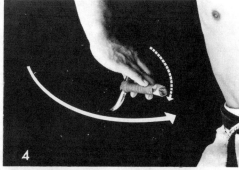

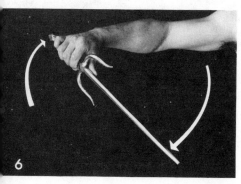

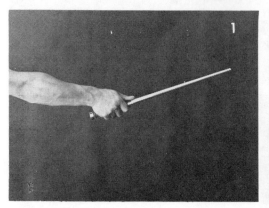

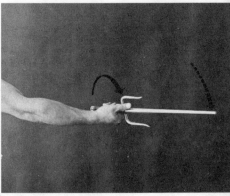

VERTICAL STRIKE

(1) Extend the sai in the blade outward position with the point very close to the target. (2) Twist your hand clockwise with the thumb side facing outward. (3) Grasp the sai loosely with your thumb and forefinger as you continue the clockwise rotation. (4) When it reaches the outside of your upper arm, begin bringing the blade over, as illustrated. (5) Continue the rotation. Prepare to strike by bringing the sai past your ear and directing it toward your target. (6) Grasp the sai firmly with all of your fingers and continue toward the target. (7) Snap your wrist and forearm into a fully extended position to apply a focused strike.

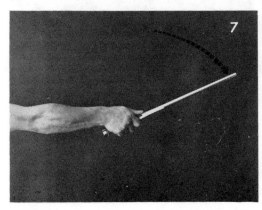

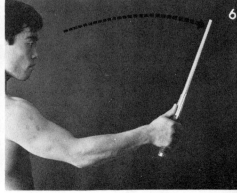

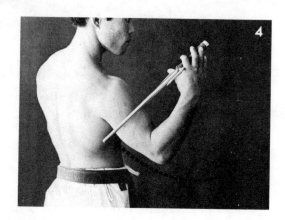

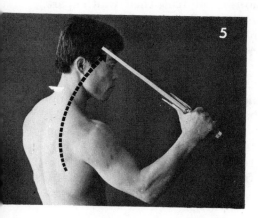

STANCES

Whether a technique is used for offense or defense, a stable base is mandatory. The stances, as well as the movements employed in the use of the sai have been adapted from karate. Through years of study, these stances have evolved to produce maximum stability and balance for thrusting, striking and parrying techniques.

The importance of the body from the waist down in making and maintaining proper stances is stressed, but stances are actually a total body concept. The position of the feet, their width apart, the bend and attitude of the knees, and the position of the head, shoulders, trunk and arms play an equally important role. A foundation of well-balanced, correct stances insures the efficiency of sai techniques.

When assuming a stance, place emphasis on keeping your back straight. Your upper torso should be correctly balanced on your hips without leaning forward or backward.

The positioning of your feet cannot be too wide or too long, otherwise the execution of your technique will be weakened. Also, a quick follow-up from an incorrect stance will be difficult if not impossible. Correct stances are fixed at a length best suited for stability and mobility.

READY STANCE
(Heisoku Dachi)

A ready position in which your feet are together and your arms are along the sides of your uniform. This position is also used in preparation for the bow.

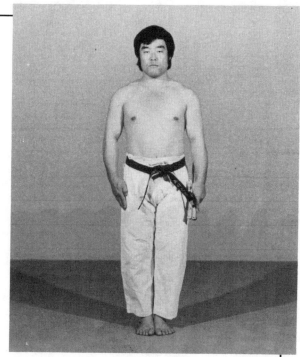

FRONT VIEW

READY STANCE
(Musube Dachi)

A ready position in which your heels are together, your toes pointed outward at 45 degree angles, and the sai are crossed in front of your body.

FRONT VIEW

FRONT VIEW

NATURAL STANCE
(Heiko Dachi)

A natural position in which your feet are spread slightly apart, and your toes are pointed forward. Extend one arm in the punching position and prepare to punch with your cocked arm.

FRONT VIEW

NATURAL STANCE
(Soto Hachiji Dachi)

A natural position similar to heiko dachi, except your toes are pointed outward. The sai are held in front of and away from your body.

NATURAL STANCE
(Uchi Hachiji Dachi)

A natural position similar to heiko dachi, except your toes are pointed slightly inward. The sai are held to the sides of your body with the blades pointing upward.

FRONT VIEW

NATURAL STANCE
("T" Dachi)

A natural position in which one of your feet is pointed forward and the other to the side in a T formation. Extend the sai of your forward arm downward, and hold the other sai palm inward at waist level. The T stance is used while awaiting your opponent's move. You can maneuver forward, backward and to both sides from this stance.

FRONT VIEW

FRONT VIEW

"V" STANCE
(Reinoji Dachi)

A natural position similar to "T" dachi, except your rear foot is pointed at a forty-five degree angle in a V formation.

SIDE VIEW

FRONT VIEW

FORWARD STANCE
(Zenkutsu Dachi)

A stance in which your forward leg is bent at the knee. Extend your other leg behind you and lock it at the knee. This position is primarily used to block and attack.

SIDE VIEW

FRONT VIEW

BACK STANCE
(Kokutsu Dachi)

The back stance is used to defend against a frontal attack. This position is also known as an extended T stance. Point your front foot forward and your rear foot, bent at the knee, to the side. Place most of your weight on your rear leg so that it may be used for support.

SIDE VIEW

CAT STANCE
(Nekoashi Dachi)

The cat stance emphasizes mobility and allows you to kick with your forward leg in combination with a sai strike. Both legs are bent at the knees. Put most of your weight on your rear leg and rest your front leg lightly on the ball of your foot.

FRONT VIEW

SIDE VIEW

HORSE STANCE
(Kiba Dachi)

The horse stance is used to defend against attacks from either side, and also for side-stepping to avoid frontal attacks. Spread your legs shoulder width apart. Bend your knees and point your toes forward.

FRONT VIEW

STRADDLE-LEG STANCE
(Shiko Dashi)

The straddle-leg stance is similar to the horse stance except your toes are pointed outward at 45 degree angles. This position provides you with better maneuverability to the side than the horse stance.

FRONT VIEW

SIDE VIEW

FRONT VIEW

CROSSED-LEG STANCE
(Kosa Dachi)

The crossed-leg stance is primarily used as a recovery position from a jump, but can also be used as a maneuvering tactic for a kick, or to pivot evasively. Cross one leg over the other with both knees bent. Place your front foot flat on the floor and support your rear leg on the ball of your foot.

SIDE VIEW

TENSION STANCE
(Sanchin Dachi)

The tension stance is primarily used for dynamic tension practice and close-in fighting. Spread your legs slightly apart, and bent at the knees, with your toes pointed inward.

FRONT VIEW

SIDE VIEW

FRONT VIEW

CRANE STANCE
(Sagiashi Dachi)

The crane stance is used to defend against footsweeps or weapon attacks to your legs. You can also deliver kicks from this position. Stand on one leg, holding it slightly bent at your knee with your toes pointed outward. Raise the leg being attacked and shift your body back out of range at the same time.

SIDE VIEW

REAR DEFENSE STANCE
(Okinawan Kokutsu Dashi)

The rear defense stance is used to retreat from an attack from the rear. Weight distribution and foot positions are the same as in the forward stance.

FRONT VIEW

SIDE VIEW

BLOCKS

To effectively block a blow or thrust from a weapon such as the bo (staff) or katana (sword), a mere movement of the arm is not sufficient. Although each member's individual function is important, the body must work as a unit, with the sai used as an extension of the body. Distance and timing also play an important role in the overall effectiveness of a block.

Blocks can be roughly divided into three major categories. You may use a strong block to subdue attacks by striking your weapon (sai) against your opponent's weapon or his arm or leg. Another type of block calls for a glancing or sliding movement which redirects the force of your opponent's technique. The glancing block will cause your opponent's weapon to slide off of the sai, allowing you to follow up much faster with an effective counter technique. The most economical method of blocking is one in which you anticipate your opponent's move, and remove yourself from the line of attack. Using this method, you can nullify his blow without indulging in any physical contact.

Keep in mind that you must never overextend a block, thus leaving yourself open for attack. All blocks terminate in a position parallel with the outer extremes of your body. This practice allows you to sufficiently deflect your opponent's technique past your body and quickly follow up with an effective counterattack.

AUGMENTED OUTSIDE BLOCK

(1) Begin with your left hand extended forward and your right hand placed over and above your left shoulder. (2 & 3) As you bring your left hand inward in front of your solar plexus, swing your right hand across your body with the sai pointing downward to complete the block.

OUTSIDE BLOCK
(Blade Downward)

(1) Begin with your left hand extended forward and your right hand placed over and under your left armpit. (2 & 3) Bring your left hand back to your waist as you swing your right hand across your body with the sai pointing downward to complete the block.

OUTSIDE BLOCK
(Blade Outward)

(1) Begin with your left hand extended forward and your right hand placed over and under your left armpit. (2 & 3) Bring your left hand back to your waist as you swing your right hand across your body with the sai pointing outward to complete the block.

INSIDE BLOCK
(Blade Downward)

(1) Begin with your left hand extended forward and your right hand raised parallel to your right ear. (2 & 3) Bring your left hand back to your waist as you swing your right hand across your body with the sai pointing downward to complete the block.

INSIDE BLOCK
(Blade Outward)

(1) Begin with your left hand extended forward and your right hand raised parallel to your right ear with the blade pointing behind you. (2 & 3) Bring your left hand back to your waist as you swing your right hand forward with the blade pointing outward and slightly upward to complete the block.

UPWARD BLOCK

(1) Extend your left hand slightly above your head in the upward block position and place your right hand at your waist. (2) As you raise your right hand upward, simultaneously bring your left hand downward and close to your body. (3) As you assume the upward block position with the blade of the sai along the inside of your forearm, place your left hand at your waist.

UPWARD X BLOCK

(1) Begin with both hands held at your waist. (2) Simultaneously bring both sai upward with the blades crossed and pointing downward. (3) Using your wrists, snap the blades upward in front of and above your head to complete the x block.

DOWNWARD BLOCK
(Blade Upward)

(1) Begin with your left hand extended forward and your right hand placed over and above your left shoulder. (2 & 3) Bring your left hand back to your waist as you swing your right hand downward across your body with the sai pointing upward to complete the block.

DOWNWARD BLOCK
(Blade Downward)

(1) Begin with your left hand extended forward and your right hand placed over and above your left shoulder. (2 & 3) Bring your left hand back to your waist as you snap the sai, held in your right hand, downward to complete the block.

KARATE AND SAI SIMILARITIES

Any karate movement may be used with the sai if you consider the sai an extension of that movement. Since most of the movements used with the sai have been borrowed from karate techniques, it is important to maintain good karate form for distance, balance and footwork.

FACE PUNCH

(1) Without a weapon, execute a standard karate forward lunge punch at the face of your opponent. (A) To perform the same punch with the sai, drive the butt of the sai directly into your opponent's face.

VARIATION

(1) Without a weapon, execute a variation of the standard karate forward lunge punch by making a finger strike to the opponent's eye. (A) To perform the same punch with the sai, drive the point of the sai into the eye of your opponent.

OUTSIDE CHOP

(1) Without a weapon, execute a standard karate shuto strike with the usual circular arc to the head or neck of your opponent. (A) To perform the same strike with the sai, strike the head or neck in the same manner, pointing the blade slightly upward.

TIGER CLAW STRIKE

(1) Without a weapon, execute a standard karate tiger claw strike with the usual straight forward motion. (A) To perform the same strike with the sai, strike your opponent's neck with the prong in the same manner, pointing the blade slightly upward.

BACK-FIST STRIKE

(1) Without a weapon, execute a standard karate back-fist strike with the usual outward arc of approach. (A) To perform the same strike with the sai, strike your opponent's face with the blade in the same manner.

ELBOW STRIKE

(1) Without a weapon, execute a standard karate elbow strike with the usual outward arc of approach. (A) To perform the same strike with the sai, you may drive the point into your opponent's mid-section by holding it tightly underneath your forearm, or you may execute other variations like (B) an upward strike, (C) a downward strike and (D) a backward thrust.

UPWARD BLOCK

(1) Without a weapon, counter a forward lunge punch to your face with an upward block. (A) To perform the same block against a bo (staff) attack, hold the sai tightly underneath your forearm with the blade downward.

UPWARD X BLOCK

(1) Without a weapon, counter a forward lunge punch to your face with an upward x block—hands either open or closed. (A) To perform the same block against a bo attack, cross the sai blades forward and upward in an x.

INSIDE FOREARM BLOCK

(1) Without a weapon, counter a forward lunge punch to your solar plexus or midsection with a clockwise inside forearm block. (A) To perform the same block against a bo attack, hold the sai tightly underneath your forearm with the blade downward.

INSIDE SWEEP BLOCK

Without a weapon, you can also counter a forward lunge punch to your solar plexus or midsection with an inside sweep block. (1-3) Bring your open knife hand around clockwise in a 180 degree semi-circle to parry your opponent's thrust. (A-C) To perform the same block against a bo attack, hold the sai underneath your forearm with the blade downward.

DOWNWARD BLOCK

(1) Without a weapon, counter a low punch to the stomach area with a downward block. (A) To perform the same block against a bo attack to your lower stomach or groin, hold the sai tightly against your outside forearm with the blade upward. (B) A variation of the downward block can be used by lifting your leg and assuming the crane stance. Block downward with the blade pointing downward.

DOWNWARD X BLOCK

(1) Without a weapon, counter a front kick to your groin with a downward x block. (A) To perform the same block against a bo attack, cross the sai blades forward and downward in an x.

KNIFE-HAND BLOCK

(1) Without a weapon, counter a forward punch to your solar plexus or midsection with a knife-hand block. (A) To perform the same block against a bo attack, snap the sai blade outward.

BASIC MOVEMENTS
WITH FOOTWORK

As you begin to combine basic footwork with the sai strikes and blocks, place the emphasis on total body coordination. Practice the following movements repeatedly until they become strong and fluid.

PUNCHING EXERCISE

(1) Begin with your left hand extended outward and your right hand held palm inward at your waist. (2-3) Punch forward with your right hand and retract your left hand back to your waist. Correct application occurs by following the exact principles of the basic punch used in karate. The only difference lies in how your hands are placed at your waist. (A) Retract your hand with the palm facing inward to avoid injury and provide smooth execution. (A1) Do not retract your hand, palm up, when using the sai. The prongs will contact the sides of your abdomen and possibly cause injury.

NOTE: This exercise (photo 3) may be performed with your left hand held palm upward or palm inward as well.

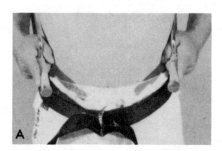

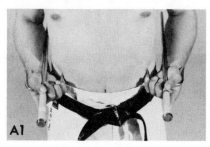

STRAIGHT PUNCH

(1) Begin the punching exercise by assuming a left foot forward stance with your left hand extended forward. (2-4) Step forward, assuming a right foot forward stance and execute a right hand punch with the butt of the sai. (5-7) Step forward, assuming a left foot forward stance and deliver a left hand punch with the butt of the sai. You can also punch with the points of the sai held outward.

UPWARD BLOCK

(1) Assume a left foot forward stance with your left hand held in a blocking position at head level. (2-4) Step forward, assuming a right foot forward stance and execute an upward block with the sai angled downward and the blade held firmly against the outside of your forearm. (5-7) Step forward, assuming a left foot forward stance, and repeat the upward block on your left side.

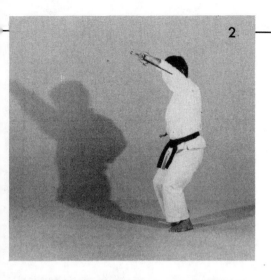

INSIDE BLOCK

(1) Assume a left foot forward stance with your left arm extended outward and bent at the elbow. (2-4) Step forward, assuming a right foot forward stance and execute a right-hand inside block with the blade of the sai held against the inside of your forearm. (5-7) Step forward, assuming a left foot forward stance and repeat the inside block on your left side.

OUTSIDE BLOCK

(1) Assume a left foot forward stance with your left arm extended forward. (2 & 3) As you step forward with your right foot, bring your right hand over and underneath your left armpit. (4 & 5) Snap your forearm and wrist into a fully extended position with the blade outward and assume a right foot forward stance. This movement can also be used as a strike to the face or head. (6-8) As you step forward with your left foot, bring your left hand over and underneath your left armpit. (9-10) Execute the outside block as you assume a right foot forward stance.

AUGMENTED OUTSIDE BLOCK

(1) Assume a right foot back stance and hold both sai forward with the points angled upward. (2 & 3) As you step forward with your right foot, place both sai back and to your left. (4) Keeping the points outward, assume a left foot back stance and bring the sai forcefully in front of your body. The use of both sai provides more power in the outside block. (5-7) Step forward with your left foot and repeat the augmented outside block on your left side.

DOWNWARD BLOCK

(1) Assume a left foot forward stance with your left hand held in a blocking position along the left side of your body. (2 & 3) As you step forward with your right foot, bring your right hand above your left shoulder. (4) Assume a right foot forward stance and execute a downward block with the blade of the sai held underneath your right forearm. (5-7) Step forward with your left foot and repeat the downward block on your left side.

OUTSIDE CIRCULAR BLOCK

(1) Assume a right foot forward stance with your right hand extended forward. (2-4) Step forward with your left foot, assuming a cat stance, and swing your left arm around in a counterclockwise circle with the sai pointing downward along the inside of your forearm. Your right hand should be placed in front of your solar plexus in a guarding position with the sai pointing downward. (5-8) Step forward with your right foot, assuming a cat stance, and repeat the outside circular block with your right hand. The outside circular block can be used to stabilize an attack by hooking the prong over your opponent's wrist or weapon.

VERTICAL ELBOW STRIKE

(1) Assume a right foot forward stance with your right hand extended in front of you. (2-4) Step forward, assuming a left foot forward stance, and snap your left elbow upward to a bent position slightly higher than your left shoulder. When executing any elbow strike with the sai, be sure to press your index finger against the handle. This will cause the blade of the sai to remain in a stable position along your forearm. (5-7) Step forward, assuming a right foot forward stance, and repeat the vertical elbow strike on your right side.

ROUNDHOUSE ELBOW STRIKE

(1) Assume a right foot forward stance with your right hand extended forward. (2 & 3) Step forward, assuming a left foot forward stance, and swing your elbow around in a clockwise semi-circle to a bent position parallel with your left shoulder. (4-6) Step forward, assuming a right foot forward stance, and repeat the roundhouse elbow strike on your right side.

HORIZONTAL ELBOW STRIKE

(1) Assume a right foot forward stance with your right hand extended forward. (2 & 3) Step forward with your left foot as you bring your left hand over and above your right shoulder. (4) Execute a horizontal thrust with the back portion of your elbow as you assume a horse stance. The striking area is the point of the sai. (5-7) Step forward with your right foot, assuming a horse stance, and repeat the horizontal elbow strike on your right side.

CIRCULAR GROIN STRIKE

(1) Assume a left foot forward stance with your left hand extended forward. (2-7) Step forward, assuming a right foot forward stance, and swing the sai around in a vertical clockwise circle until it is extended forward at your own groin level. (8 & 9) Continue the circular rotation, retracting the sai back to the inside of your forearm. (10-19) Step forward, assuming a left foot forward stance, and repeat the circular groin strike on your left side.

NOTE: Even though this technique is called the "circular groin strike," you have the option of hitting any variety of targets such as the chin or midsection as you pass these areas during the movement.

CONTINUED

COMBINATIONS

When practicing combinations, try to develop balance and accurate footwork with the various sai techniques. Combine different movements until the combinations are fast and smooth. When you practice for speed, however, be careful not to sacrifice the accuracy of the techniques. You may have to try different stances since stances that are strong and balanced in single movements may not be as effective in combined activity.

Good technique stems from good form. Students of the sai often attempt to move on to the next technique before finishing the preceding movement. Do not forget that the ideal technique is perfect in form and places you in a balanced position for the next move.

The combinations contained in this chapter provide the reader with a large assortment of both defensive and offensive techniques. The student must keep in mind that the variety of combinations is infinite. Practice the combinations shown here until you have perfected them, then blend the individual movements into new combinations on your own.

LUNGE PUNCH COMBINATION I
(With Horizontal Strike)

(1) Assume a left foot forward stance with your left hand extended forward. (2 & 3) Step forward, assuming a right foot forward stance and execute a right hand punch with the butt of the sai. (4 & 5) Bring your right hand over and underneath your left armpit. (6 & 7) Snap your right forearm and wrist into a fully extended position to execute a horizontal strike. (8 & 9) Using inside retraction, draw the sai back to your forearm in the blade inward position. (10-22) Step forward, assuming a left foot forward stance, and repeat the combination on your left side.

LUNGE PUNCH COMBINATION II
(With Horizontal Strike and Downward Block)

(1) Assume a left foot forward stance with your left hand extended forward. (2 & 3) Step forward, assuming a right foot forward stance and execute a right hand punch with the butt of the sai. (4) Raising your left arm over your throat, simultaneously bring your right hand over and underneath your left armpit. (5 & 6) Snap your forearm and wrist into a fully extended position to execute a horizontal strike. (7 & 8) Using inside retraction, draw the sai back to your forearm in the blade inward position. (9 & 10) Bring your right hand over and above your left shoulder, and execute a downward block with the blade of the sai held underneath your right forearm. (11-21) Step forward, assuming a left foot forward stance, and repeat the combination on your left side.

LUNGE PUNCH COMBINATION III
(With Horizontal Strike, Vertical Strike and Downward Block)

(1) Assume a left foot forward stance with your left hand extended forward. (2 & 3) Step forward, assuming a right foot forward stance and execute a right hand punch with the butt of the sai. (4) Bring your right hand over and underneath your left armpit. (5 & 6) Snap your forearm and wrist into a fully extended position to execute a horizontal strike. (7 & 8) Twist your hand counterclockwise with the thumb side facing outward. (9 & 10) Continuing the rotation in a full circle, snap your forearm and wrist into a fully extended position to execute a vertical strike. (11 & 12) Using inside retraction, draw the sai back to your forearm in the blade inward position. (13 & 14) Bring your right hand over and above your left shoulder, and execute a downward block with the blade of the sai held underneath your right forearm. (15-28) Step forward, assuming a left foot forward stance, and repeat the combination on your left side.

CONTINUED

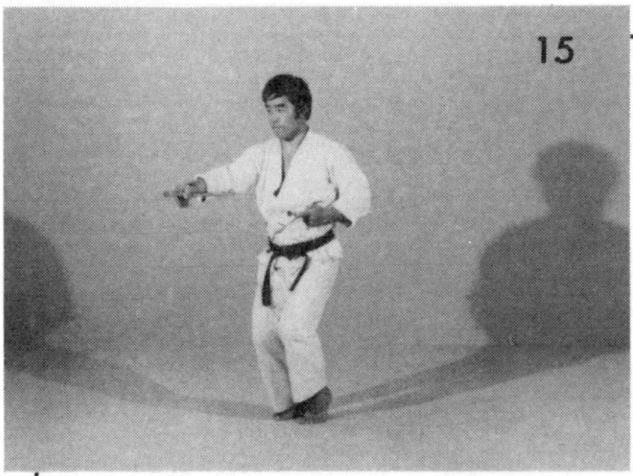
15

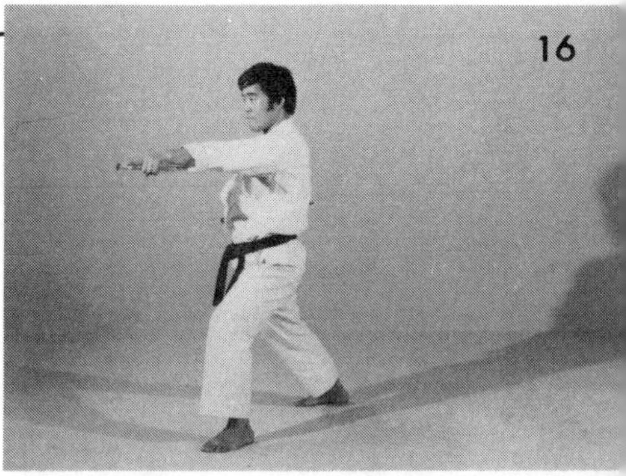
16

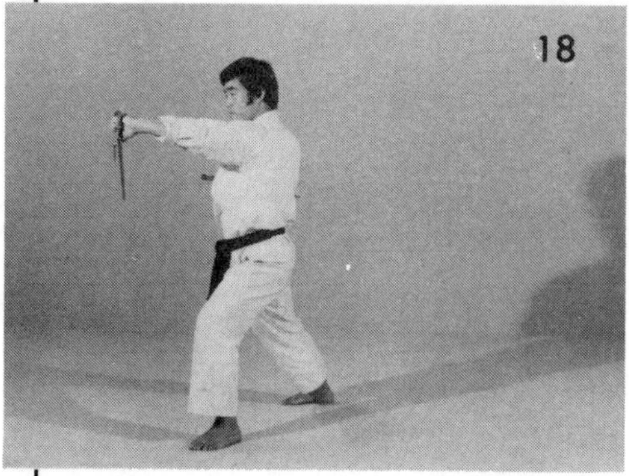
18

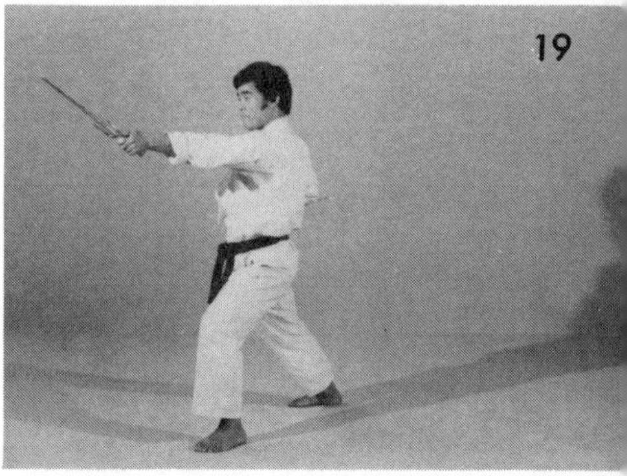
19

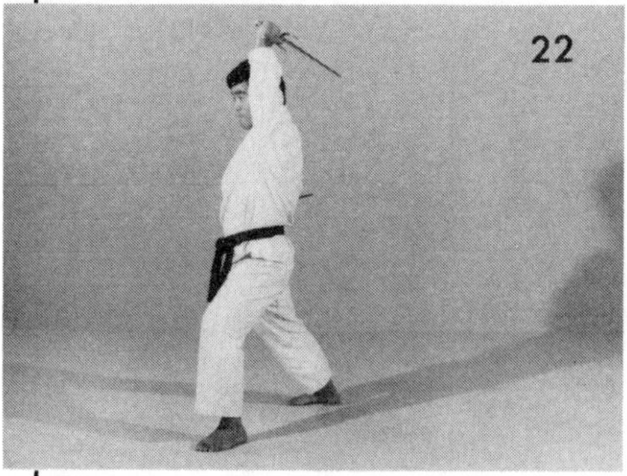
22

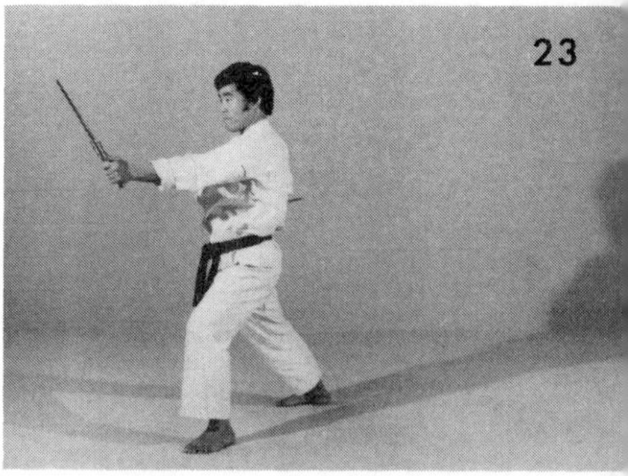
23

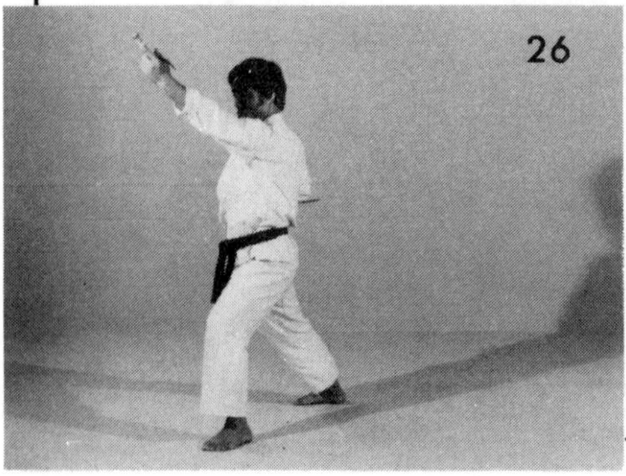
26

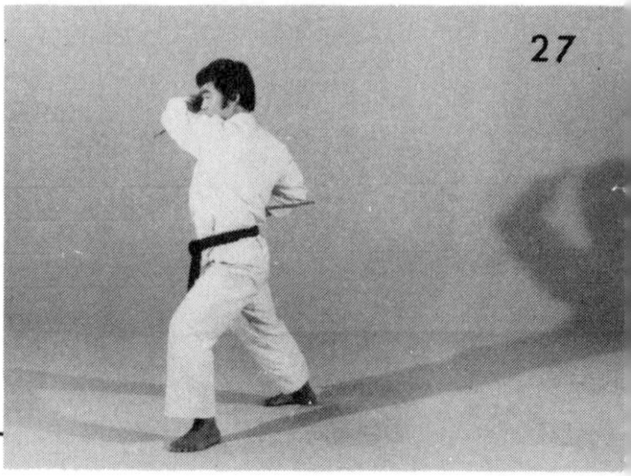
27

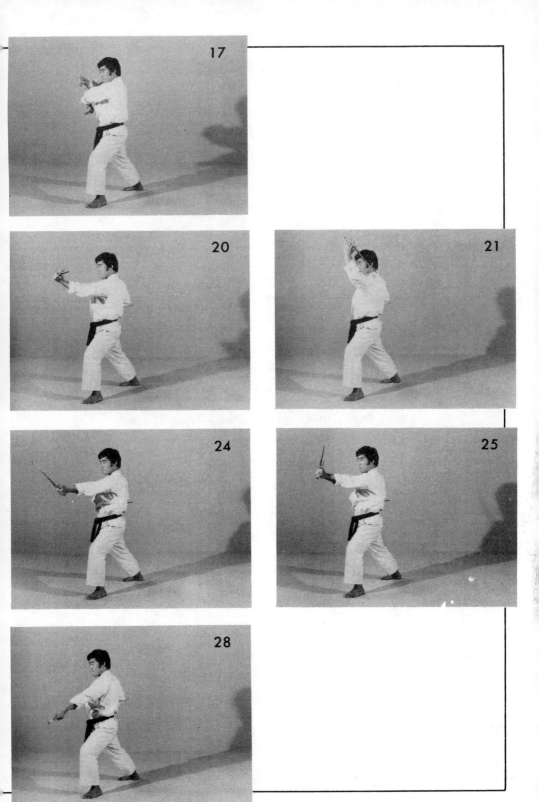

BACKHAND COMBINATION I
(With Inside Chop)

(1) Assume a right foot forward stance with your right hand extended forward. (2-4) Step forward, assuming a left foot forward stance, and execute an inside chop with your left hand. (5 & 6) Slide your left foot outward to assume a horse stance, bring your left hand over and above your right shoulder, and execute a backhand strike with the blade of the sai. (7-11) Step forward, assuming a right foot forward stance, and repeat the combination on your right side.

BACKHAND COMBINATION II
(With Inside Block and
Two Horizontal Elbow Strikes)

(1) Assume a natural stance (soto hachiji dachi). (2 & 3) Step forward, assuming a left foot forward stance, bring your left hand up to your left ear, and execute an inside block with the sai pointing downward. (4 & 5) Slide your left foot outward to assume a horse stance, bring your left hand over and above your right shoulder, and deliver a horizontal elbow strike with the point of the sai. (6-8) Bring your left arm back and execute a backhand strike with the blade of the sai. (9 & 10) Using overhand retraction, draw the sai back to your forearm, and (11) deliver another horizontal elbow strike. (12-23) Step forward, assuming a right foot forward stance, and repeat the combination.

CONTINUED

14

15

18

19

22

23

DOUBLE BLADE STRIKE I
(With Double Hook Block)

(1) Assume a natural stance (soto hachiji dachi). (2 & 3) Step forward with your left foot as you cross the blades of the sai above your head. (4 & 5) Assume a forward stance as you swing the sai around and deliver a double blade strike in front of you. (6) Using overhand retraction, draw the sai back to your forearms. (7 & 8) Bring the sai forcefully downward in a double hook block as you lean your weight backward to assume a back stance. The double hook block is used to trap your opponent's wrists with the sai prongs in a grabbing attack, or to trap a thrusting attack of the bo. (9-14) Step forward, assuming a right foot forward stance, simultaneously crossing the blades above your head. Repeat the combination.

DOUBLE BLADE STRIKE II
(With Double Outward Block and Front Kick)

(1) Assume a natural stance (soto hachiji dachi). (2 & 3) Step forward with your left foot, assuming a back stance, cross your arms, then push both arms forcefully outward with the blades downward. This double block is used when your opponent grabs you from the front. (4 & 5) Execute a front kick with your left foot. (6 & 7) As you retract your kick, cross both sai above your head. (8 & 9) Step down, assuming a left foot forward stance, and execute a double blade strike. (10 & 11) Using overhand retraction, bring the sai into a blade downward position. (12-22) Step forward, assuming a right foot forward stance, and repeat the combination.

SPARRING

As one of Okinawa's classic hand-to-hand combat weapons, the sai is a versatile and highly effective means of defending against long range attacks. Since the sai was traditionally developed as a defensive weapon against the bo or katana, the illustrations contained in this chapter begin with blocking techniques before demonstrating the various counterattacks. Also included is a section dealing with the sai as a defensive weapon against nunchaku, which demonstrates the blocking techniques and counterattacks as well. Within these combinations, you will recognize the basic techniques covered in previous chapters. It is mandatory to perfect the basics in order to effectively defend against weapon attacks.

Obviously, the variations of basic movements in free sparring are endless. Therefore, the weapons student must shrewdly judge the validity of alternating the prescribed combinations. For instance, a front snap kick may be substituted for a roundhouse kick when the situation would indicate such an alternate choice. However, such variations should not induce the student to neglect the rigid practice of classic basics indicated in the illustrations. It is from these basics that the art of the sai has originated and developed.

CAUTION: The sparring techniques simulated here are for instruction only. Students should never attempt live sparring against an opponent.

UPWARD BLOCK I
(With Reverse Punch Counter)

(1) Assume a right foot forward stance with the sai held outward in a sparring position. (2 & 3) As your opponent attacks with an overhead strike, place your right foot back and execute a left-hand upward block with the sai blade pointing downward. (4-6) Hook the prong of the blocking sai over the bo to pull it past your body as you deliver a reverse punch to your opponent's face with the butt of your right-hand sai.

VARIATION

(A) An alternate counterattack can be used by snapping the sai outward and (B & C) thrusting the point at your opponent's eyes, neck or stomach.

VARIATION

(X) You can also counter by bringing the sai upward and (Y & Z) striking your opponent's neck or head with an inside chop.

UPWARD BLOCK II
(With Double Punch Counter)

(1) Assume a right foot forward stance with the sai held outward in a sparring position. (2 & 3) As your opponent attacks with an overhead strike, place your right foot back and execute a right-hand upward block with the sai blade pointing downward. (4 & 5) Hook the prong of the blocking sai over the bo to pull it past your body, and (6) deliver a lunge punch to your opponent's face with the butt of your left-hand sai. (7 & 8) Immediately follow-up with a right-hand reverse punch with the butt of the sai.

VARIATION

To complete the technique, you may either (A) deliver a second lunge punch to your opponent's lower face with your left-hand sai, or (B) follow up with a right-hand reverse punch with the butt of the sai.

UPWARD BLOCK III
(With Outward Deflection
and Vertical Strike)

(1) Assume a left foot forward
stance with the sai held outward in
a sparring position. (2 & 3) As your
opponent attacks with an overhead
strike, place your left foot back as
you snap your right-hand sai outward to perform an upward block.
(4-6) Push the sai to your right,
deflecting the bo past your body.
(7 & 8) Raise the sai above you and
snap the blade forward to strike
your opponent's head.

UPWARD BLOCK IV
(With Wrist Hook and Horizontal Elbow Strike)

(1) Assume a right foot forward stance with the sai held outward in a sparring position. Grip the right-hand sai by the blade. (2 & 3) As your opponent attacks with an overhead strike, place your right foot back and execute a left-hand upward block with the sai pointing outward. (4 & 5) Trap the bo between the prong and blade of the blocking sai as you place the right-hand sai around the outside of your opponent's extended wrist. (6) Pull sharply downward on the right-hand sai, hooking your opponent's wrist and deflecting his arm past the right side of your body. (7 & 8) While retaining the hook position, bring your left hand over by your right ear, then deliver a horizontal elbow strike with the point of the left-hand sai.

UPWARD X BLOCK I
(With Double Blade Strike and Prong Thrust)

(1) Assume a right foot forward stance with the sai held outward in a sparring position. (2 & 3) As your opponent attacks with an overhead strike, place your right foot back and execute an upward x block. (4 & 5) Snap both sai out to the sides, knocking the bo past your body with the left-hand sai. (6) Prepare to execute a double strike to your opponent's neck.

VARIATION

(A) From step 6, you may either execute a double blade strike to the neck, or (B) a double prong strike to the neck.

122

2

3

5

6

B

UPWARD X BLOCK II
(With Inside Chop and Prong Thrust)

(1) Assume a right foot forward stance with the sai held outward in a sparring position. (2-5) As your opponent attacks with an overhead strike, place your right foot back and execute an upward x block. (6) Hook the bo between the blade and outside prong of your left-hand sai as you cock the right-hand sai behind your head. (7-9) Push downward on the left-hand sai, knocking the bo past your body as you execute an inside chop to your opponent's neck with the right-hand sai. (10) Thrust the prong of your right-hand sai into your opponent's neck.

UPWARD X BLOCK III
(With Front Thrust Kick)

(1) Assume a right foot forward stance with the sai held outward in a sparring position. (2-4) As your opponent attacks with an overhead strike, place your right foot back and execute an upward x block. (5-7) Keep the sai in the x block position as you raise your right foot and deliver a front thrust kick to your opponent's midsection.

127

INSIDE SWEEP BLOCK I
(With Backhand Strike and Horizontal Elbow Strike)

(1) Assume a left foot forward stance with the sai held outward in a sparring position. (2 & 3) As your opponent attacks with a forward thrust, step back with your left foot and execute a right-hand inside sweep block to deflect the bo past your body. (4) Assume a horse stance as you bring the right-hand sai over to your left shoulder. The left-hand sai should be placed under your right armpit. (5 & 6) Deliver a backhand strike to your opponent's face with the right-hand sai. (7-12) Retract the right-hand sai to your forearm, cock your hand past your left shoulder and execute a horizontal elbow strike to your opponent's face.

INSIDE SWEEP BLOCK II
(With Combination Counter)

(1) Assume a left foot forward stance with the sai held outward in a sparring position. (2 & 3) As your opponent delivers a forward thrust, step back with your left foot and execute a right-hand inside sweep block to deflect the bo past your body. (4-6) Cock the right-hand sai back to your left shoulder and deliver a backhand strike at your opponent's head. (7) Your opponent blocks the backhand strike with a two-hand upward thrust of the bo. (8-10) Quickly take advantage of his exposed targets by sliding your rear foot toward your right and delivering a right-foot side thrust kick to your opponent's midsection. (11-14) Retract your right foot, assume a right foot forward stance, and deliver a left-hand reverse punch with the butt of the sai. (15-17) Retract your left hand and execute a spear thrust with the point of your right-hand sai to your opponent's stomach.

INSIDE SWEEP BLOCK III
(With Horizontal Elbow Strike)

(1) Assume a left foot forward stance with the sai held outward in a sparring position. (2 & 3) As your opponent delivers a horizontal strike, step back with your left foot to assume a horse stance and sweep both sai to your left to block the attack past your body. (4) Trap the bo between the prong and blade of the left-hand sai as you extend your right hand back past the left side of your body. (5 & 6) Deliver a horizontal elbow strike to your opponent's neck.

UPWARD BLADE BLOCK
(With Rotation Defense)

(1) Assume a right foot forward stance with the sai held outward in a sparring position. (2 & 3) As your opponent delivers a two-hand overhead attack, thrust both sai forward with the blades upward to check the attack. (4) Push down on the left-hand sai as you hook the outside prong of the right-hand sai around the bo. (5-7) Rotate the sai in a counterclockwise circle until the bo strikes your opponent's groin. (8-10) Bring your right hand back, and thrust the butt of the sai into your opponent's face.

135

OUTSIDE SWEEP BLOCK
(With Front Thrust Kick
and U Punch)

(1) Assume a right foot forward stance with the sai held outward in a sparring position. (2 & 3) As your opponent executes a forward thrust, step back with your right foot to assume a cat stance and execute an outside sweep block with the left-hand sai to deflect the bo past your body. (4 & 5) Cock your left foot and deliver a front thrust kick to your opponent's midsection. (6-9) Retract your left foot, assume a left forward stance, and simultaneously execute a u punch with the butt of both sai. Your right-hand sai should be directed toward your opponent's face while your left strikes him in the midsection.

HORIZONTAL X BLOCK
(With Combination Counter)

(1) Assume a right foot forward stance with the sai held outward in a sparring position. (2 & 3) As your opponent attacks with a reverse horizontal strike, step back with your right foot and execute a horizontal x block toward your right side. (4-6) Your opponent sweeps your left leg at the knee with the opposite end of the bo, causing you to turn and expose your back. (7-9) He then steps forward, places the bo over your head and applies a choking technique. (10 & 11) Retract the sai to your forearms and (12) execute a backward elbow strike to his midsection with your left-hand sai. (13) Strike your opponent's eyes with the butt of your right-hand sai.

DOWNWARD BLOCK I
(With Leg Sweep and Two Hand Thrust)

(1) Assume a right foot forward stance with the sai held outward in a sparring position. (2-4) As your opponent attacks with a reverse leg sweep, lift your right leg to assume a crane stance as you execute a downward block with the right-hand sai. (5 & 6) Extend your right foot forward and sweep your opponent's front foot toward your left. (7) As he falls to the ground, lift both sai above your head with the points downward, and (8 & 9) execute a two-hand downward thrust to your opponent's neck and back areas.

141

DOWNWARD BLOCK II
(With Side Thrust Kick
and Backhand Strike)

(1) Assume a left foot forward stance with the sai held outward in the sparring position. (2-4) As your opponent attacks with a reverse leg sweep, step back with your left foot and execute a right hand downward block with the sai blade pointing upward. (You can also use an alternate step by lifting your right leg to assume a crane stance while you block, as seen in photo 4A). If you wish to continue this downward block technique through the side thrust kick and backhand strike, do as follows: (5) Strike your opponent's knee with your side thrust kick. (6-9) As your opponent's knee sinks to the floor, raise your right sai overhead and deliver a backhand strike to his head or neck.

DOWNWARD X BLOCK
(With Upward X Block
and Roundhouse Kick)

(1) Assume a right foot forward stance with the sai held outward in a sparring position. (2 & 3) As your opponent attacks with a groin strike, step back with your right foot and execute a downward x block. (4 & 5) Your opponent counters the block with an overhead strike. Block this follow-up with an upward x block. (6 & 7) Raise your right foot and execute a roundhouse kick to his head.

2

4

5

7

DISARMING A
THREATENING OPPONENT

(1) Assume a left foot forward stance with the sai blades pointing toward you. Grip the right hand sai by the blade. (2-4) As your opponent stands ready to attack, execute a horizontal strike with the left-hand sai. (5) When the sai blade contacts the bo, it will cause your opponent to lose his grip. (6-8) Reach forward with the right-hand sai, hook the inside prong around your opponent's knee, and (9) pull backward until your opponent falls to the floor. Follow-up with any practical and effective technique for the situation.

SINGLE SAI DEFENSE

(1) Assume a right foot forward stance with the right-hand sai held outward in a sparring position. (2 & 3) Your opponent quickly strikes the right-hand sai with the end of the bo, causing you to drop the sai. (4-6) As your opponent recocks the bo and steps forward to deliver an overhead strike, execute an upward block with the left-hand sai. (7 & 8) Hook the outside prong around the bo and pull downward as you grasp the center of the bo with your right hand. (9-11) Snap your arms forward and downward, striking your opponent's neck with the opposite end of the bo. Continue exerting the downward pressure until you drive him to the floor. (12 & 13) Cock the bo back and thrust it straight forward into your opponent's midsection.

NOTE: If you elect, you may execute a simple throw after you have grasped hold of the bo (photo 8) without striking your opponent's neck with the opposite end of the bo.

OVERHEAD CIRCLE DEFENSE

(1) Assume a right foot forward stance with the sai held outward in a sparring position. Grip the left-hand sai with the blade resting against your forearm and pointing downward. (2-4) As your opponent delivers an overhead circle attack, block outward with the blade of the left-hand sai as you raise your right-hand sai in preparation to counter. (5-7) Execute an inside chop to your opponent's neck with the right-hand sai.

REVERSE SHOULDER
SWING DEFENSE

(1) Assume a left foot back stance with the sai held blade downward along your forearms. (2-4) As your opponent delivers a reverse shoulder swing attack, flip both blades outward and perform a double upward block. The outside prong of the left-hand sai should block the attack while the right-hand sai blade contacts the nylon cord of the nunchaku. (5) Trap the cord between the blade and prong of the right-hand sai by tilting the sai and twisting your body counterclockwise. (6) Disarm your opponent by forcefully pulling the sai to your left. (7-9) As the nunchaku drops behind you, pivot to your right and strike your opponent's throat with the blade of the right-hand sai.

SIDEARM DEFENSE

(1) Assume a right foot forward stance with the sai held blade downward along your forearms. (2 & 3) As your opponent attacks with a sidearm swing, execute a left-hand downward block with the sai blade pointing upward. (4) Flip the right-hand sai blade outward and (5) drive the point into your opponent's midsection. (6) Retract the right-hand sai and raise the weapon overhead. (7 & 8) Bring the outside prong down over his extended wrist, taking him down on one knee and causing him to drop the nunchaku. (9) Step back with your right foot as you apply clockwise pressure with the prongs on your opponent's wrist. (10) Place your right knee on the floor and take him down completely to a prone position.

NOTE: If you elect, you may finish the technique with the driving of the sai point into your opponent's midsection (photo 5) rather than following through with the final attacks.

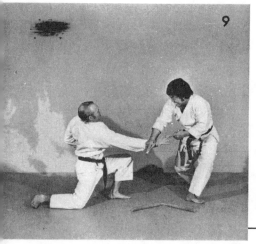

CROSS SWING DEFENSE

(1) Assume a left foot forward stance with the sai held blade downward along your forearms. (2-4) As your opponent delivers a low cross swing attack, lift your left leg to assume a crane stance as you execute a downward block with the left-hand sai. (5 & 6) Place your left foot down and execute a horizontal sweep crossing in front of your opponent's chest with the blade of the right-hand sai. (7) Strike your opponent's right wrist, knocking the nunchaku from his grasp. (8 & 9) Bring your right foot forward, sweeping your opponent's forward leg to the left. (10 & 11) As he falls, raise the blade of the right-hand sai and strike him on the back of the head or neck.

FIGURE EIGHT DEFENSE

(1) Assume a left foot back stance with the sai held blade outward in a sparring position. (2-4) Avoid your opponent's initial swing by moving your torso to the left. (5-8) As he swings around to complete the figure eight strike, time the attack and use an inside chop with the right-hand blade to deflect it past your body. (9-12) After completing the block, slide your left foot closer and deliver a side thrust kick with your right foot to your opponent's throat or midsection. (13) Step forward with your right foot, assuming a horse stance, and bring your right hand over past your left shoulder. (14-16) Execute a backhand strike to his throat, knocking your opponent to the floor.

CONTINUED